RIFLEMAN/DOCTOR

A MARINE CORPS PHYSICIAN'S MEMOIR

WARREN S. GILBERT, MD

CDR-FMFQO, MC, USN-Ret.
Commanding Officer, 4th Marine Division, 4th
Medical Battalion, STP WC-2, Ret.

iUniverse LLC
Bloomington

RIFLEMAN/DOCTOR
A MARINE CORPS PHYSICIAN'S MEMOIR

iUniverse books may be ordered through booksellers or by contacting:

iUniverse
1663 Liberty Drive
Bloomington, IN 47403
www.iuniverse.com
1-800-Authors (1-800-288-4677)

Because of the dynamic nature of the Internet, any web addresses or links contained in this book may have changed since publication and may no longer be valid. The views expressed in this work are solely those of the author and do not necessarily reflect the views of the publisher, and the publisher hereby disclaims any responsibility for them.

Any people depicted in stock imagery provided by Thinkstock are models, and such images are being used for illustrative purposes only.
Certain stock imagery © Thinkstock.

ISBN: 978-1-4917-3067-6 (sc)
ISBN: 978-1-4917-3066-9 (e)

Library of Congress Control Number: 2014905960

Printed in the United States of America.

iUniverse rev. date: 04/11/2014

CONTENTS

PREFACE

Every branch of the armed forces has its' own dedicated, inclusive medical personnel. Every branch, that is, except the Marine Corps. The Navy and the Marine Corps are both branches of the Department of the Navy. All of the medical services in the Marine Corps are provided by Navy personnel on a voluntary basis. You see, the Marine Corps is strictly a fighting 'Force of Readiness'; 'First to Fight', as the saying goes. Ready to go anywhere in the world, anytime, almost on a moment's notice, due to its' prepositioned MAGTFs (Marine Air Ground Task Forces) that are strategically situated throughout the world ready to deploy in support of any combat mission.

Anyone who serves with the Marine Corps, including medical personnel, have to be trained, prepared, and ready to be a part of the fighting force that is placed in harm's way as the need arises. Hence, there are scant medical resources in the Marine Corps, limited to those who are willing to do just that, in contrast to most medical personnel who serve in the other military branches where that eventuality is much less likely.

This book chronicles what it is like to be a physician serving with the Marine Corps, in all of its' aspects, not the least of which being involved in combat operations where your life is on the line under some of the most austere conditions imaginable. I spent most of my military career doing just that, as an emergency trauma specialist serving with the 4th Marine Division. This is my story.

DEDICATION

This book is dedicated to the men and women of the armed forces of the United States of America who I have had the honor and privilege of serving with during my years of military service; and to all who have paid the ultimate price in giving their lives in defense of our Country.

FROM ROUGHNESS TO REGIMENTATION

There are many reasons why an individual would choose to go into the medical field. This could range from the lure of monetary gain to the more altruistic ideal of wanting to help people, or make the world a better place, or find a cure for disease, and anything in between. For me it was not all that complicated. From an early age I was a rather mischievous, active child who had his share of injuries for which I would be seen by our pediatrician. I discovered a certain fascination for what he, and other doctors, did and how they could resolve my medical problems with medication, suturing of my assorted wounds, and removing my tonsils so I no longer had repeated ear infections and sore throats.

As I progressed in school I found that the two subjects that I excelled in, and the only ones that I really had any interest in, were math and science. I, therefore, knew that if I was to go to college in the hope of elevating myself out of the rough neighborhoods of the Southside of Chicago, and go on to some sort of meaningful, successful, career it would either be as a teacher or a doctor. Teaching was out of the question because it might mean that I would end up with the kind of students that I went to school with, myself included, who were constantly getting in trouble, disrupting class, and seemingly impossible to reach and impart with knowledge. That left either research (too boring, laborious, repetitive and frequently unsuccessful) or medicine.

My family was not affluent. My father worked long hours, sometimes at more than one job, and made enough for our lives to be reasonably comfortable but without much extra money to go around. I had a paper route from the time that I was ten years old until I got a job at the local hardware store at age thirteen. I worked there for several years after school, when I wasn't at football practice, and on weekends. I learned some very practical skills that would help me land a job in construction work once I turned sixteen and could afford my own beat-up used car and insurance.

My high school was in a ghetto and was a melting pot of minorities, mostly black and Hispanic, which weren't really minorities since they outnumbered the white kids. In order to survive you had to be either tough, play sports, or know members of the various gangs in order to avoid getting mugged on the long walk home after school. I chose all three. Having developed an affinity for weight lifting around age thirteen, by the time I entered high school I was close to six feet tall and quite muscular. I took up boxing and football in high school and, as such, guys didn't mess with me. When I would walk home after football practice it was generally dark and I would usually get approached by one gang or another at some point during that journey. If I knew some of the gang members they would just let me pass. If I didn't than I would end up fighting my way out of the situation and sprinting off to home. It was not uncommon for me to be involved in one fight or another several times per week, both in and outside of the school. As a result of boredom, and to maintain my cred with the less than socially desirable element in our school, I got into trouble on a fairly regular basis. I was never destructive or abusive but I was a lippy smartass and would oftentimes disrupt class prompting a trip to the principal's office. This, along with certain pranks that I pulled-off while at school resulted in my being suspended several times. At least once my father had to intervene on my behalf to prevent me from getting expelled.

I was a veritable genius in comparison to 80% of the other students and found that I could get really good grades by just showing up to class and doing at least some of my homework. As a result, I had a good enough grade point average to get into college. I desperately wanted to get out of Chicago. During the fall of my senior year of high school, in the midst of our football season, I was approached by a scout from one of the fraternities at Drake University in Des Moines, Iowa. He told me that if I attended college at Drake, and agreed to play football for the fraternity, he could guarantee me a place in their Pledge Class without my having to even go through the fraternity rush process. This sounded very inviting so I applied, and got accepted, to Drake University. I took out student loans to pay for school and got a job working in the biology department as a lab assistant so I would have some spending money, since I was there on my own dime. It was truly culture shock for me, as I began college life, having come from a lower middle class area of Chicago to this ivy-league school whose students (myself excluded) were all driving late model cars and enjoying their $2000/month expense allowances from home.

Being a star on the fraternity football team, as a freshman, I was like a kid in a candy store. There were beer blasts and parties every weekend and I was having a great time. The only problem was that I was bigger and stronger than most of the fraternity members, including the active members. My rough edges would show through at the beer blasts when I would get drunk and, on more than one occasion, beat the crap out of one of my fraternity brothers. That type of behavior was not generally tolerated, particularly coming from a pledge, but we were winning intramural football so the fraternity officers let it slide. However, once football season was over I was approached in my dorm room by six fraternity members, probably hoping there would be safety in numbers, who informed me that I had been blackballed from the fraternity. This obviously upset me and certainly did not aid in my already less than stellar study habits. My first year of college was a bust but was also a wake-up call to me that I needed to turn my life around if I ever expected to amount to anything. Starting with my sophomore year I knuckled down and got straight A's in my classes going forward. After three years of pre-med courses, working in the biology dept., assisting in labs, and doing hundreds of dissections of many different animals, I was ready to apply to medical school.

Rush Medical College, which was the first medical school in the United States, was reopening its doors after being closed for one hundred years. They were only going to admit 66 medical students to the first new class and they were looking for a diverse assortment of individuals rather than just a bunch of egghead 4.0 brainiacs. With my hard luck upbringing, combined with my varied sports history and self-supporting work ethic, I was just the kind of person they were looking for, and so I was accepted. Once again, I obtained a student loan to cover tuition and housing. As luck would have it, our anatomy professor was looking for an assistant to help him in the lab portion of our anatomy course. He administered an initial anatomy proficiency exam to our class and I scored so high on the exam, from the years that I spent working in the biology lab at Drake, that I was able to proficiency out of the lab portion of the course. I was also hired by the professor to assist him in teaching the lab portion of the course to my fellow students as well as work for him in the dissection lab. He tasked me with performing total body dissections of the muscular, neurologic and vascular systems and creating a library of slide presentations that the students could access to help them in their dissection work on cadavers, and to prepare for practical exams.

Since we were a new crop of house staff at the medical center we were at the beck and call of the residents and attending staff. They were an excellent source of knowledge for us and we were their workhorses on the medical units. I had finally found my niche. Medicine became my passion. I soaked it up like a sponge and just couldn't get enough. Due to my proficiency in anatomy and dissection work I had a natural leaning towards the surgical field. The problem was that I enjoyed every aspect of medicine and did not want to necessarily restrict my practice of medicine to any one narrow scope. So I gave my all to every clerkship and clinical rotation.

When I was on a rotation, such as obstetrics, if there were students on that rotation who were not at all interested in OB/GYN, such as those who had already decided what branch of medicine that they were going to pursue, I would take their on-call nights and pull extra shifts. That way I would get to perform more deliveries and become as proficient as possible in that field. The same held true for other rotations which meant that I did not get a great deal of sleep but, in turn, I gained a great deal of knowledge. One of the residents that I worked under once called me hyper-efficient. Fortunately, I had never required much sleep, which really proved to come in handy in the years to follow. All of my elective rotations were spent in emergency medicine and surgery while I continued my training in the core clerkships. The surgeons that I trained under during my clerkships and elective rotations were so impressed with my surgical abilities that during my senior year in medical school I was actually placed on the rotating intern call schedule, and functioned as an intern, taking call along with the surgical residents and performing surgeries with them during my nights on-call.

By the time I was ready to apply for residencies I had already sub-interned in surgery but decided on a residency in Family Practice with additional training in emergency medicine and surgery. The skills that I obtained while in medical school gave me such a good knowledge base that I sailed through residency and was appointed Chief Resident in my last year. Upon completion of my Family Practice residency I was appointed as the Medical Director of the trauma ER at the medical center where I did my residency and was granted general surgery privileges at the hospital, as well. I was the only resident coming out of a Family Practice residency to be granted general surgery privileges in a Chicago area hospital without having gone through a formal surgical residency. Additionally, I was offered a partnership position with an older family physician to join his practice, which I did. So for the next six years I practiced family medicine, including OB and pediatrics, ran the trauma ER (which additionally included working at least twelve shifts per month), and performed general surgery. By 1983 I was so burned out by the knife and gun club in the ER, and my insane work schedule, that I needed a change. Coincidentally, the hospital administrator decided that he wanted to really upgrade the status of the ER and ordered me to fire all of the existing doctors currently working for me in the ER, which included several of my colleagues who had been in residency with me, and hire only Board Certified ER physicians in their place. I refused and gave him three months notice at which time I quit what I was doing and left to start a new medical group at another hospital. That did not work out as I had intended and I became very disillusioned after two years. There was a family physician from Reno, Nevada that I had known for around eight years through a medical ski meeting that I attended every year at Lake Tahoe. He knew that I loved that area of the Country and when he was considering winding down his practice he thought of me and called to see if I might be interested. I made a trip out West to look at his practice and the region. It was just what I was looking for so, in May of 1986, I moved my family to Reno, NV to make a fresh start.

ANSWERING THE CALL

I was actively practicing family medicine, had opened a second office, was working some sporadic ER shifts, became very active with the Reno Rodeo Association, and became politically active in the Nevada Academy of Family Physicians. As you have probably surmised, I tend to get involved in a great deal of activities, stay rather busy, and am always up for a new challenge. In addition to all of my professional work and the Rodeo Association, I was an avid skier, worked out regularly, and was very active in my children's lives as a supporter and coach in their various sporting activities. I met my wife, Debby, when I started on my first rotation in the ER as a resident. She was one of the trauma nurses in the ER and I was immediately drawn to her due to her incredible nursing skills, not to mention her captivating beauty and personality. We were both married at the time but ultimately both got divorced, not as a result of any relationship between us. We subsequently got seriously involved and we married within a couple of years of my completing my residency training. When we moved to Nevada she initially stayed at home to care for our children, particularly our infant daughter, Anna, and within several years assumed the position of nurse/manager of the Employee Heath Service at John Ascuaga's Nugget Hotel and Casino where she has continued to work for the past 24 years.

I had also moved our family from our house to a small ranch, bought us all horses, and got more and more personally involved in the rodeo- and my older daughter, Gina, and my second oldest, Joey, in junior rodeo. My youngest daughter, Anna, also got involved in horsemanship and all three children had become experienced gymnasts. As they progressed through school Anna participated in track and played basketball, soccer and rugby; Joey played soccer and football, and ultimately boxed for the University of Nevada-Reno boxing team (where I was on the coaching staff) winning three back-to-back NCBA national championship boxing titles. He went on to win the State Golden Gloves middleweight title and then turned pro. At the height of his pro career he was ranked the number three middleweight in the world but decided to retire from boxing after a significant head injury when he was thirty-five. He had gone to law school during the time that he turned pro so when he retired from boxing he devoted his fulltime effort towards his law career. Gina gravitated from junior rodeo and gymnastics towards personal fitness and nutrition and ultimately became a certified personal trainer who is one of the most sought-after trainers in Reno. Anna, who majored in psychology and literature at UNR, used those skills to write a column for the Reno Gazzette-Journal and co-author a book on self-empowerment and women's issues. She currently is in a management position at ARC Health and Wellness where I am the Medical Director. My oldest daughter Melissa, from my previous marriage, had stayed in Chicago when I moved to Nevada. She pursued her passion of a career in law enforcement and became a police officer. I mention all of the above to emphasize the point that I have always impressed upon my children the importance of staying physically fit and getting involved in as many activities as possible to challenge yourself, both mentally and physically, and to strive to persevere and excel no matter what the odds—with or without me. I have also ingrained in them the importance of maintaining a profound love of our great Country and pride in being an American. It is something that I am passionate about and they have been exposed to my patriotic spirit throughout their lives. This has shone through in their personal and professional achievements and indomitable spirits and can-do attitude. They have been incredibly supportive, and demonstrably proud, of my military service and the example that I have strived to give to them. I am very close to my children and they are an integral part of me and everything that I do. Aside from the personal pride and sense of accomplishment that I garnered through my military service a huge motivating factor in all that I do is to be a good father to them and a symbol of what it truly means to be an American.

After the Embassy bombing in Beirut, the first Gulf War, and the first World Trade Center bombing, it became clear that the Middle East was becoming a real hotbed of terrorist activity and an increasing threat to all people and nations of non-Muslim faith, particularly the United States. With things heating up in the Middle East I seemed to be getting contacted on a fairly regular basis by the Army, Navy and Air Force imploring me to join the Armed Forces, either on an active duty or Reserve basis, due to the need for qualified physicians. My wife was a busy nurse manager at John Ascuaga's Nugget Hotel/Casino. My children were well-established with their circle of friends and their school, career and extracurricular activities and I was, once again, getting somewhat bored with my structured, now monotonous, routine. My Country seemed to be calling me for some reason or higher purpose.

I made the decision to join the Naval Reserve, rather than going active duty, because it would allow me to maintain my current lifestyle and would only involve my serving the Navy one weekend per month and two weeks per year on a training exercise.....or so I thought.

Things seemed to be going rather well. I was assigned the collateral duty of Training Officer for my medical detachment in addition to my primary duties as a medical provider at our Reserve Center during drill weekends. Fortunately, the Reserve Center was located just north of Reno so it was only a twenty-minute drive for me to make on drill weekends. Our medical unit was there to medically support the other co-located military Reserve units which included the 4th Force Marine Reconnaissance Unit. For the most part we spent our drill weekends performing physicals, keeping all of the military personnel up to date on their blood work and immunizations, and treating any injuries that might occur during training over the weekend. It was not particularly exciting, or challenging, but I enjoyed the camaraderie and it gave me a sense of pride that I was helping to do my part for my Country. Then came 9/11.

OFF TO WAR

I remember standing in my bedroom, getting ready for work on the morning of September 11, 2001 when I got a call from a friend in Chicago telling me to turn on the news because a plane had flown into one of the Twin Towers at the World Trade Center in New York City. I, like many of you probably did too, turned on the television fully expecting to see that an errant small plane had flown into the building, as has happened a number of times in the past in various cities. When the reporter stated that it had been a commercial airliner that had hit the tower I became somewhat more concerned. That is a much more unexpected scenario and had never happened before that day. My thought was that the pilot either lost total control of the aircraft or something mechanically serious had gone acutely wrong. As they were still reporting on the incident I watched as the second plane flew into the other tower. Now my worst suspicions had been confirmed..... this was clearly a pre-meditated terrorist attack. I became instantly enraged and as the morning unfolded, and the other two planes crashed into the Pentagon and the field in Pennsylvania, my anger grew.

Over the ensuing months I underwent some significant personal changes. I became much more anxious and quick to fly off the handle than was typical for me. I could not get the events of 9/11 out of my mind and all I could think about was getting revenge on the bastards who did this to us, and doing whatever needed to be done to insure that this would never happen again. The ongoing thoughts were ever-present to the point where my wife and family were making comments about my changed personality. I was able to function at work and at home but I thought about it throughout the day, and it was on my mind when I first awoke each morning and when I attempted to go to sleep at night; even waking me up during the night and ruining my sleep. As the war with Iraq became more and more imminent I became more and more anxious at the prospect of the U.S. finally taking the fight to the terrorists to their home turf to neutralize the threat at its' source and, hopefully, prevent another attack on our soil. To my wife's constant chagrin, I was glued to the television every night watching the cable news network and keeping an eye on the ticker tape going across the bottom of the screen with its constant updates on the prospect of war. One evening I was sitting on the couch with my wife, Debby, and the ticker tape read something like "30,000 reservists anticipated to be called up to war with Iraq." My wife turned to me and said, "Goodbye." Four days later, on March 30, 2003, I got a call from my Reserve Center notifying me that I had been issued orders for deployment and had two days to report for pre-mobilization processing. As I hung up the phone a calm came over me that I had not felt since September 11, 2001. I was finally going to get to exact my measure revenge that I had sought for almost two years.

For anyone who is not familiar with the mobilization process it is rather laborious and time-consuming.....usually. Once the decision has been made, by the Command element of a military branch, to include a service member in the personnel assets of a particular deployment 'orders' are generated and issued to that service member. These 'orders' include, among other things, the reporting date, where to report, the starting and ending date (if known) of the deployment, and as many specifics of the mission as possible along with travel arrangements, etc. The service member usually has knowledge of a pending mobilization, anticipates the receipt of his or her 'orders', and has some time to prepare for the upcoming deployment. Again, I say.....usually. When the decision was made to invade Iraq there was no such preparatory period. When I received the call to report to our

Reserve Center within two days it was basically to condense a 3-5 day mobilization process down to one day. I went to the Reserve Center, was handed my 'orders', made any updates to my service record and emergency-type information, and was told to go home and get my gear together because I was leaving in two days and had to report to Fleet Command at Naval Hospital-Bremerton within three days. There was not even enough time to generate an airline ticket. I had to drive my personal vehicle from Reno to Seattle, WA in order to get there in time for the deployment to begin. This, obviously, did not give me much time to notify my employer that I was leaving or to say goodbye to my family and friends. So I packed up my sea bags and back pack, threw them in the back of my pick-up truck, and took-off for Seattle.

I mobilized with the primary Naval Fleet Hospital, out of Bremerton, Washington, that was responsible for the trauma casualty care of our wounded service members. In the first six weeks of the war the Fleet Hospital treated around 670 casualties and performed around 250 surgical procedures. My deployment lasted six months and, although it was not a true combat deployment, I had put in many days of long hours and ended up receiving a Navy and Marine Corps Commendation Medal for my efforts. It was certainly more exciting and challenging than my usual medical activities during reserve drill weekends but it was still just basically Navy medicine, not unlike what I was used to doing in the civilian world. When I returned home several things happened which were to change my life forever.

AND SO IT BEGINS

I was sitting in my living room watching television one evening in November, 2003 when the phone rang. My wife answered it and called out to me saying, "Some admiral is on the phone and wants to speak with you." I jumped off of the couch and grabbed the phone since it is not every day that you receive a phone call from an admiral. It was Admiral Peter Andrus calling to inform me that I had been chosen as the recipient of the AMCON (Association of Medical Corps Officers of the Navy) Award for 2003. I said, "What is the AMCON Award?" He laughed and told me that each year a committee of admirals review the nominations, from all of the Commands across the Country, of those officers below the rank of Commander, who their Command feels are the best in the Naval Reserve. I was a LCDR (Lieutenant Commander) at the time and, unbeknownst to me, I had been nominated by my Command. Admiral Andrus mentioned that it was quite an honor to be chosen as the best junior officer in the Naval Reserve. He then said that in reviewing my file he noted that I had an extensive background of ER trauma, and surgical experience, and asked if I would consider switching from Navy medicine to join Program 9. I asked, "What is Program 9?" He again laughed and informed me that Program 9 is the Reserve medical branch of the Marine Corps and is comprised of Naval physicians, PAs (Physician Assistants), nurses, corpsmen, and other naval personnel that provide the medical care, and service support elements, to the 4th Marine Reserve Division through the 4th Medical Battalion. I said that it sounded interesting and I would certainly consider it. He added that someone from the 4th Med BN (4th Medical Battalion) would contact me soon to follow-up on our conversation.

The following weekend, when I arrived for drill at the Reserve Center, I was called into the CO's (Commanding Officer's) office and informed that our co-located 4th Marine Recon Unit had requested that I be cross-assigned out to them as the OIC (Officer In Charge) of their medical detachment. They had heard about the work that I had done during my deployment and wanted someone with my experience to head-up their medical unit. I eagerly agreed to do so because it was a very locked-on (well-disciplined, well-trained, proficient in all things) Marine unit that spent most of its drill weekends in the field doing combat, weapons, and demolition training or on Blackhawk helicopters doing parachute training, night operations and practicing various combat operations scenarios. I received some very valuable training from them over the next several months that would prove to come in handy very soon.

Within the first month that I had joined 4th Force Recon I was contacted by the 4th Med BN and formally asked to join Program 9, which is headquartered at MCAS (Marine Corps Air Station) Miramar, just north of San Diego. I agreed to do so if they would allow me to continue to drill with the 4th Force Recon Unit. They agreed to let me stay cross-assigned out to 4th Force Recon as long as I drilled once a quarter at Miramar. I said that would be fine with me. But there was something else in store for my future.

DEPLOYMENT AS A COMBAT EMERGENCY TRAUMA SPECIALIST

I had spent three consecutive drill weekends in the field with 4th Force Recon. One combat operations exercise included M-16 rifle and M-9 pistol live fire training. Another involved Blackhawk helo night-ops combat exercises. The third entailed demolition training where we practiced making various types of explosive charges for different purposes, from anti-personnel mines to blowing up bridges or other structures. Within a month of returning from the third field-ex, in early March of 2004, I received a phone call from a CAPT Boggelin, the XO (Executive Officer) of 4th Med BN, who proceeded to tell me that I was being put on notice that I would be receiving orders, within the next few weeks, for a combat deployment. I said to him, "Are you aware that I have only been home six months since returning from my deployment with OIF-3 (Operation Iraqi Freedom-2003)?" He said, "Yes, I do, but this is a very high-profile mission that had to be approved by the CNO (Chief of Naval Operations) at the Pentagon and signed-off by President Bush. We really need someone with your trauma and surgical background." I asked, "Where am I being deployed to?" I was told that "I cannot divulge that, as yet, but it is somewhere in the sand. When the mission details are completed I will have more information for you." Then he told me he would be in touch soon but in the meantime I was not to say anything to anyone about this.

Having been blind-sided by a mere 2-day window to get all of my gear together for my last deployment I had since become much more organized. Since returning home from that deployment I converted an old, no longer functional, freezer (the kind that lies flat and has the lift-up door) into my gear locker. By keeping my gear all in one place, and having it organized and pre-staged, I can virtually be ready to leave for anywhere within a matter of a couple of hours. The only variable is how much, and what type, of clothing to pack in my sea bags, depending on where in the world we are being deployed, and for how long.

Two weeks passed before I heard back from him at which point he outlined what the mission would entail. Afghanistan was preparing for its first democratic election in history, to take place in September. The Taliban was in full force trying to prevent the elections and coerce the Afghan people into not voting, under threat of death. They were infiltrating all of the cities and towns throughout Afghanistan in order to strong-arm their efforts. The U.S. was sending the 22MEU/SOC (Marine Expeditionary Unit/Special Operations Capable) as part of a CJTF (Combined Joint Task Force) to set-up a remote firebase in the middle of the desert in Southern Afghanistan just north of the Pakistan border and approximately 70 miles northwest of Kandahar. The plan was for the MAGTF (Marine Air Ground Task Force) to access whatever intel they could and conduct convoy missions into the various towns and villages in Southern Afghanistan, as well as into the surrounding mountain regions, in order to seek out and neutralize the Taliban threat. My role was to command an STP (Shock Trauma Platoon) that would attach to the ground infantry forces in the desert and provide acute casualty care, in combat, as the casualties occur.

An STP is a specialized, mobile, combat trauma unit that is self-contained. It has its own personnel consisting of one or two ER trauma physicians, one PA, one trauma nurse, ten to twelve corpsmen, and six Marines to drive our vehicles, provide COMM (communications), and provide on-site security for the area where we set-up our trauma and holding/evacuation tents and where we provide our medical treatment. The STP has its own vehicles including a 5-ton truck for hauling gear, tents and personnel, 2-HUMVEE ambulances, 1-high-back HUMVEE for carrying supplies and personnel, a trailer to haul all of our medical supplies, and a generator to provide our electrical power. The STP is the primary warfare combat medical support for the Marines that are deployed to remote FOBs (Forward Operating Bases). The STP sets-up its tents and equipment in proximity to the Command tent and not far from the bivouac site so its members can respond quickly to incoming casualties. There is a treatment tent, where the acute care is administered, and a holding tent for casualties who are post-treatment and either awaiting discharge back to their unit or helicopter medevac to a base with surgical or other specialty capability. At the entrance to the treatment tent there is a triage area established to evaluate incoming casualties as they arrive at the STP and determine priority of care. As soon as the STP is set-up and operational the next order of business is to establish the trauma teams. Each team would consist of a medical provider (generally the trauma docs and the PA) along with 2-3 corpsmen. Each trauma team is assigned to its own trauma station and proceeds to that station at the time of a mass casualty (multiple casualties arriving to the STP at the same time) and provide care to the casualties as they are brought to their station. There are generally 3-4 trauma stations in the treatment tent, each fully equipped to render emergency trauma care to casualties. The trauma nurse is generally in charge of the triage process and then would help coordinate the treatment flow, handle pharmacy/medication issues, monitor any casualties that had to be intubated and placed on a ventilator, and oversee the medivac process.

It is important to note that the STP corpsmen are not clinicians. On the civilian side they may be fire fighters, police officers, teachers, construction workers, truck drivers, or any of a variety of occupations. But they are not medical personnel, per se, and the medical care that they are called upon to participate in while being a part of the STP is solely a product of what they are taught during their training with the STP. That is why I stressed training as heavily as I did throughout my years as the commanding officer of the 4th Marine Division's primary STP. During every drill weekend we would spend a portion of that weekend in the classroom with me presenting different briefs on combat medicine. One of the most important of these was my brief on 'Trauma Fundamentals' which was intended to help them recognize certain clinical signs that would indicate that a casualty was in need of urgent medical attention by a physician. Included in the brief were what I called my 'oh shit' numbers, e.g. HR (heart rate) less than 60 or greater than 120, RR (respiratory rate) less than 10 or greater than 20, systolic BP (blood pressure) less than 90 or greater than 160, a GCS (Glasgow Coma Scale) less than 13, etc. Without going into detail here, these types of parameters would allow a corpsman to determine, within a minute or so of an initial assessment of a casualty, if that casualty was in need of immediate physician intervention or could wait. This was particularly important during triage of multiple casualties, arriving simultaneously, to prioritize which were in the most urgent need of medical attention. By doing serial re-assessments of the casualties awaiting treatment the corpsmen could funnel the most critical casualties to me as I became available to care for them. More on this later. Additionally, several drill weekends per year would be devoted to field exercises where we would convoy to a site, set-up the STP equipment as we would in a combat scenario, and do STP training, most importantly involving mass casualty training with simulated victims.

When there are combat missions, either up into the mountains or into a town, one of the trauma physicians goes on the convoy, along with several corpsmen, and the other stays behind to man the STP at the firebase for any casualties that may be flown in by helo. In between combat missions the entire STP is available for any casualties that may be sent there from other operations going on in the region from one of the other units in the JTF (Joint Task Force). It is generally either feast or famine. When there is activity in the region, with ongoing combat missions, then the STP may receive numerous casualties, of varying severity, and often 6-10 at a time. This is referred to as a mass casualty. The purpose of the STP is to stabilize acute injuries, perform life-saving procedures such as inserting chest tubes, controlling hemorrhage, obtaining IV access to give blood and medications, partially repairing extremity wounds from gunshots, shrapnel or blast injuries, etc. We sometimes have to intubate severe injuries so they can be rendered unconscious by medication, given via RSI (Rapid Sequence Intubation) and placed on a ventilator in order to perform some of these life-saving procedures, or for transport to a higher echelon of care in order to receive needed surgical intervention. The STP does not have the capability to actually perform surgery, since we do not have operating rooms or anesthesiology, but can do everything up to surgery. Since I have a surgical background the intent was to use me in that capacity, as well, if the need arose. Again, more on that later.

The concept of STPs arose as a result of Vietnam. In all wars, up to and including Vietnam, the major cause of death on the battlefield, for those not killed instantaneously, was blood loss. There is something commonly referred to in trauma circles as the 'golden hour'. This is, basically, that time period post-injury during which, if appropriate medical care is not provided, the patient will die. Roughly 95% of those service members who died of their wounds did so because they did not receive life-saving medical treatment within that first hour. Since the routine use of STPs in combat has been undertaken the reverse is true. We are able to save 95% of casualties that are alive at the time that we initiate treatment. This is due to the fact that we are either right there on the combat mission when the casualty occurs or are within a short helo ride from the firefight, and there are always several members of the STP on every combat mission.

As you may or may not be aware, when individuals join the armed forces they swear an oath to protect and defend the United States from all enemies, foreign and domestic. Everyone does this as a matter of course, but the Marine Corps takes it to another level. When you serve with the Marine Corps you also swear to uphold and adhere to six Codes of Conduct:

I am an American, fighting in the force which guards my country and our way of life. I am prepared to give my life in their defense.

1. I will never surrender of my own free will. If in command, I will never surrender the members of my command while they still have the means to resist.
2. If I am captured I will continue to resist by all means available. I will make every effort to escape and to aid others to escape. I will accept neither parole nor special favors from the enemy.
3. If I become a prisoner of war, I will keep faith with my fellow prisoners. I will give no information nor take part in any action which might be harmful to my comrades. If I am senior, I will take command. If not, I will obey lawful orders of those appointed over me and will back them in every way.
4. When questioned, should I become a prisoner of war, I am required to give name, rank, service number, and date of birth. I will evade answering further questions to the utmost of my ability. I will make no oral or written statements disloyal to my country, or its allies, or harmful to their cause.
5. I will never forget that I am an American, fighting for freedom, responsible for my actions, and dedicated to the principles which made my country free. I will trust in my God and in the United States of America.

Please read those again, paying special attention to numbers 1, 2, and 6. Although you swear to uphold all 6 of the codes, when you go into combat with the Marines, especially into areas of the world such as Iraq and Afghanistan where terrorists and insurgents do not acknowledge, nor adhere to, the Geneva Convention, codes 3 through 5 are not an option. So when you go into combat there are only two options—survive, hopefully after a successful mission, or die. There is nothing in between.

OFF TO WAR... AGAIN

Several days after my phone brief with CAPT Boggelin I received the anticipated call from my Reserve Center that my orders had arrived and I needed to get to the Miramar Marine Base ASAP because the embarkation date had been moved up due to increased terrorist activity by the Taliban. When I arrived at Miramar for pre-mobilization out-processing I was introduced to the rest of my STP trauma team, none of whom had ever served together on deployment. We were briefed by the 4th Med BN CO, CAPT Rom Stephens, and told that we were all hand-picked by our various Commands for this high-profile mission and we only had five days to get to know each other and get all of our paperwork, gear, and immunizations in order before we were to leave for Afghanistan. So basically, I had to acquaint myself with, assess the general competency of, and coordinate the organization of a group of service members that I had never met before and, more importantly, not had the opportunity to train with, as a unit, in preparation for going into a hot combat zone where we had no idea what we may face. This provided me with no small amount of anxiety, to say the least. The one saving thought that I had was that each member of this unit had been specifically chosen for their skill in their particular field of expertise and, as such, did not require any major pre-deployment training in that regard. The 22ndMEU had already left Cherry Point by float and were en route to Kuwait where they would then be flown to Kandahar to meet up with us.

During our five days of preparation, before departing for Afghanistan, we spent time getting to know each other and comparing notes on our backgrounds and level of training and experience. I conducted several briefs for our corpsmen on combat medicine and trauma fundamentals and put them through a mini workshop in suturing and emergency airway procedures such as intubation and cricothyroidotomy, which entails making a tiny incision and placing a narrow catheter into the trachea in the neck just below the Adam's apple to obtain an emergency airway in an individual who cannot be intubated for reasons such as facial trauma. Beyond what immunizations I had previously gotten when I deployed for Operation Iraqi Freedom, we received any necessary immunizations including anthrax, typhoid, meningioccal, and smallpox. Having already received numerous vaccinations during my previous deployment all I needed was the smallpox vaccination and an anthrax booster. We also spent part of two days on the pistol and rifle range honing our shooting skills.

There is something else that you need to know about serving with the Marines. EVERY Marine is a rifleman. It doesn't matter what your MOS (Military Occupational Specialty) in the Marine corps may be, whether it is infantry, medical, culinary, mechanic, admin, etc., you are a rifleman first. Everything else is secondary (hence the title of this memoir). If you are unable to pass your yearly 9MM pistol and M16 weapons qualifications, maintain the required body standards, and pass the twice-annual PRT (Physical Readiness Test), you are administratively separated from the Marines—no exceptions. In the case of medical personnel, and corpsmen, you would be booted out of Program 9 (green-side medical) and returned to the Navy side of the house (blue-side medical). Fortunately, I have always maintained my shooting skills since a teen and have always kept in good physical condition throughout my life by playing baseball, football, hockey, boxing, skiing, biking, rock climbing, weight training.

After accomplishing as much as we could possibly fit into five days, we were ready to make the long journey to Afghanistan via

Germany and Italy (for refueling) , Tajikistan, where we spent one day at Manas Air Base, and then to Kandahar. We spent two days at the base in Kandahar before being flown forward by helicopter to what was going to be our firebase, to be named FOB Ripley.

CASUALTY CARE IN THE COMBAT THEATRE

The CH-46 helicopter dropped us off in the middle of the desert surrounded by nothing but sand, which was really not sand but more like dirty confectioner's sugar. Every step you took this fine, powdery sand sort of billowed up, like walking on the moon. There was a mountain range approximately two miles to the north of us, in the shape of a wide horseshoe, and the nearest town, Tarin Kowt, was around twenty minutes southeast of us via convoy. The two most striking things about Afghanistan, at this time of year, were the oppressive heat and the stark, austere geography. It was truly like another world and the most barren landscape I have ever seen. The temperature was never below 120 degrees during the day and was usually closer to 125 degrees. Kandahar was southeast of us and it was generally 10 degrees warmer. There was only brief cloud cover twice that I remember between April and August. We were going to be there over the period of the year known as the '120 days of wind'. What that meant was that there was a constant breeze blowing during the day, which normally would have been inviting, but basically just blew the powdery sand in the air. As a result, we breathed it, ate it, and were always dusty. At any time of the day if you were to pat your BDUs (Battle Dress Utilities, or cammies) you looked like Pigpen in the Peanuts comic strip. What it also meant was that for approximately two hours every afternoon there was a hellacious sand storm that was so vicious that you could barely see your hand in front of your face. You had to seek shelter or risk getting blown into something, and it felt like our tents were going to be uprooted and blown away. Even if we were inside our STP tents there was dusty sand blowing around inside the tent. Our equipment was always dusty and in need of being cleaned repeatedly throughout the day, as well as necessitating sweeping out the tents two to three times per day.

What you have to realize is that we were literally sitting in the middle of the desert with no perimeter protection and no hard structures. As soon as our boots hit the sand most of the BLT (Battalion Landing Team) took off for the mountains, in all directions, to hunt for bands of Taliban. There were roughly 900 service members in the JTF and our STP was the only trauma unit in all of Southern Afghanistan, with the next highest level of care, including surgical capability, being Charlie Med at Kandahar which was an hour helo flight away. There were a number of simultaneous combat missions that were initiated almost on day one to kick-off the 1st phase of Operation Mountain Storm. I sent the other ER trauma specialist in my STP on one of the missions and I stayed behind to get the STP set-up and prepare to start taking on casualties. That left approximately 100 Marines, and our STP, to establish our firebase and fend for ourselves against enemy attack. We were pretty much sitting ducks until we could establish some semblance of a firebase. My unit had to set-up our two Base-X STP trauma tents and get all of our equipment, supplies and meds arranged as per our usual SOP (Standard Operating Procedure) so we could be ready for business. The 22nd MEU had its own BAS (Battalion Aid Station) attached to it which was there to handle day-to-day sick call, non-emergent medical issues. It was comprised of a general medical doctor and a small contingent of corpsmen. My STP was there to provide the trauma care. The Marines dug out some rudimentary perimeter lookout posts and surrounded them with sandbags for some protection from small arms fire. It took all of us roughly six weeks, working mostly between combat missions, so there was more personnel to help, in order to erect a HESCO barrier wall around the perimeter of what was now FOB Ripley. HESCO barriers are plastic containers, held together by wire, which expand out in an accordion fashion, and open at the top so they can be filled with sand, dirt and rock. They provide a six-foot tall, three-foot wide wall to absorb small arms fire, shrapnel from mortars, and a barrier to penetration by the enemy. The Command Element had several large GP (General Purpose) tents of their own to house all of their communications equipment, war room, planning and briefing space and headquarters base of operations for the battalion CO, LtCol Braden. Concertina wire, with its tiny razor-sharp projections, was strung out around every individual working area such as our STP, the Command tents, and the COMM center which included our satellite dish, large antennas and radio operators, as well as around the entire perimeter of our tiny firebase. In the midst of all of this we were putting in roughly 18-hour days, not counting the nights when we were called out of our rack to treat casualties. It was so hot during the day that, even if you wanted to, you could not get into your tent until it cooled down to a balmy 90 degrees, or so, at night. If you dared to keep your tent flaps opened during the day for ventilation you would have a thick layer of dusty sand in your tent to deal with so we just kept our tents closed up until we could finally crawl into our sleeping bag around 2200 hours. The only shade that we had during the day was that which was provided by cammie netting that was strung out from the side of our trauma tents and held up by poles.

During this 6-week time period the enemy fired mortar rounds at us from the base of the mountains every few nights. We would answer back with 155mm Howitzer rounds and 50 caliber machinegun fire. Since this would occur during the night it usually meant I would be up the rest of the night. When a mortar hits within 50-100 yards of you it really rocks your world; and when debris is raining down on your little two-man tent after a mortar explodes that is a little too close for comfort. The two 155 Howitzers were located within 50 yards of our bivouac area and when they went off the sound was deafening. Although the enemy would usually come down from the mountains, quickly fire off a mortar round, and then head back up into the mountains, they were getting more and more accurate in their aim- and closer and closer to their targets.....us.

The entire BLT had set up all of our tents in one bivouac area so it looked like a sea of 2-man tents. As the mortar rounds seemed to be getting closer to us each time, we were all instructed to pull up our tents and bulldozers were brought in to dig big trenches, roughly 4 feet deep, that would accommodate no more than 12 tents. The dirt/sand that was dug up was dumped in a horseshoe shape around the trench to absorb shrapnel in the event that a mortar landed in one of the trenches. The reasoning was that it would be better to lose potentially 24 Marines with a direct hit in one of the trenches, as opposed to possibly 50 or more if a mortar were to land in the sea of tents as they were originally configured. We called them graves. So the sea of tents was converted into roughly 40 of these trenches/graves making it rather hard to navigate your way to your tent at night since there was absolutely no light other than our tiny red or blue pocket lights which barely provided enough light to see several feet in front of you. The purpose of using these muted lights was intentional so as to make you as unlikely a target as possible for snipers. In that regard, the most dreaded time of the month for us was when there was a full moon because it was huge and lit up the desert very nicely for a sniper. During that time of the month we spent as little time out in the open at night as possible and moved very quickly when we were in plain sight.

There were absolutely no amenities available to use, such as laundry facilities, showers, or any running water, for that matter. The water that we filled our canteens with was ROWPU (Reverse Osmosis Water Purification Unit) water. This is produced by drilling a well down to a water source and pumping the water up through the above purification process and then storing it in huge canvas bladders that lie on the ground in the hot desert. Water was drawn out of the bladders and transferred into 250 gallon metal holding tanks on wheels, called water bulls, which were placed in several locations on the firebase for us to access and fill our canteens. These were also out in the open so, although the water was actually fairly potable, it was always warm, at best, and sometimes even too hot to drink until it cooled off a bit once it was in our canteens. Since there were no showers, the only way that we had to 'bathe' was to strip down and stand inside a large metal storage container, called a quad-con, and pour water over ourselves using a canteen cup. There was almost no point in even doing this because five minutes after you left the quad-con you were already hot and dirty again. Although you would sweat, due to the extreme heat, there was zero humidity so the sweat would soak into your undershirt and immediately evaporate leaving a white salt residue on your shirt. The same was basically the case for attempting to wash our clothing. We would wash them out in one bucket, rinse them out in another bucket, and then hang them out to dry. Due to the dry heat our clothes would be completely dry within a very short time. However, due to the constant dusty sand blowing all around, the clothes would be dry but with a layer of dust on them. We would just shake them out and put them back on. In essence, we were always hot and dirty.

For the first two months or so all we had to eat were MREs (Meals Ready to Eat) which are an assortment of pre-packaged meals that are sealed in a plastic pouch. The 'entrée' is inside in a foil pouch. There is a plastic sleeve that contains a heating element inside into which you slide the 'entrée' and add a small amount of water to activate the heating element. After around ten minutes you remove the foil pouch, tear it open, and eat the meal. In addition to the 'entrée' there are other items included in the package such as cookies, various pound cakes, apple sauce or some other fruit concoction, raisins, pretzels, nuts, power bars, etc., all in their own individual vacuum-sealed foil pouch. By trial and error you would figure out which MREs contained the most palatable 'entrees' (or least offensive tasting) and which contained the best supplemental snack items. After a couple of months a makeshift chow hall was built out of wood and large tarps with plywood tables at which we could stand and eat. At this point we actually had a small kitchen facility that provided a very rudimentary breakfast and supper for us which was at least a break from the MREs that we now only had to eat at lunchtime.

We had no exchange on the firebase so we had to rely on packages from home for any other kind of food items, magazines, books, personal care items, basically anything that you would want to purchase- if there was any place from which to purchase it. When any of us would get a package from home we would pool our goods and share them amongst ourselves. The same would hold true for the goodwill packages that we would receive from various military support groups. Unfortunately, since we were so remote from everything, we only received mail once a month or so. Needless to say, we were all pretty lonely and homesick, and anxiously awaited anything that we would get from our families.

There were multiple combat missions involving convoys into the mountains and into various 'towns' within Oryzgun Province, all of which required medical assets. Myself and the other trauma physician would alternate going on the missions so there was always a physician at the firebase. Since I was the firebase surgeon, as well, I took care of the more critical casualties and on a number of occasions, after stabilizing casualties, I would fly with them by CH46 (Chinook helicopter) or CH53 (Sea Knight helicopter) to Kandahar and stay to help out in surgery at Charlie Med. After one or two days I would fly back to FOB Ripley. I went on approximately ten convoy missions over a period of around four months, some into the mountains and some into the tiny villages or towns which were varying distances from our firebase. While our Marines would go throughout the towns looking for Taliban I would speak with one of the elders, through an interpreter, and offer to provide humanitarian medical assistance to any needy Afghanis, along with the several corpsmen that I would bring with me, utilizing whatever meds and equipment that we would bring with us. On a couple of occasions I brought the MEU BAS Chief Petty Officer, HMC Baker, along with us to act as an additional 'medical provider' since the females often refused to see a male doctor (or were forbidden by their husband to see one). Afghan women are considered the property of the Afghan men and have virtually no say in anything. The young women are basically used as barter for goats, sheep and cattle in exchange for being given up to another male as his wife. HMC Baker was a very good looking woman and on one occasion we had just arrived at Tarin Kowt, via convoy, to provide medical care. One of the village elders approached me accompanied by one of our interpreters. As he pointed to HMC Baker, who was standing some distance away from us, he asked, through the interpreter, "How many goats would you take for that woman?" I respectfully declined his offer telling him that I was not at liberty to give her to him since she was not mine to give. He acknowledged with a nod and walked away. I went up to HMC Baker and told her of his proposed offer at which point she became rather angry but held her temper. I had all I could do to keep from laughing and she made it quite clear that she did not want the subject brought up again…...ever.

We would commandeer a building, establish a security perimeter with a small security force, and my XO, LT Brian Allen, would corral the throng of awaiting Afghanis, triage them as best as possible, and funnel them to a choke point where they would be checked for weapons, then sent into our building for treatment. We would proceed to evaluate and treat upwards of 200 men, women and children over a 5-hour or so period of time. The only medical conditions that we were really capable of treating, given our lack of available supplies, were musculoskeletal problems, various infections (mostly oral and skin), and lots of dysentery. So we gave out a lot of motrin, antibiotics and anti-diarrheals. There were some severely ill individuals that presented to us but for whom we could offer little hope or care. There were a number of individuals, however, who had potentially treatable conditions but only if they could be offered urgent surgical intervention. LT Allen was able to make contact with surgeons in Egypt and Pakistan who agreed to perform the surgeries free of charge if we could arrange transport to and from their countries. We were successful in making those arrangements on several occasions. This type of medical intervention was commonly referred to as a MEDCAP (Medical Civilian Aid Program). It was a form of humanitarian assistance that the Navy provided to needy countries around the world during peacetime. Ours were the first, that I am aware of, that were ever undertaken while at war and during combat operations.

The majority of the casualties that we treated were from gunshot wounds, RPGs (Rocket Propelled Grenades), IEDs (Improvised Explosive Devices), Cobra AT-1 attack helicopter missiles (enemy casualties incurred during a firefight), vehicle accidents and heat exhaustion/heat stroke. The casualties were pretty much split 50/50 between our Marines and enemy forces. Any casualties that occurred from combat operations within a thirty-minute helo ride from our firebase were sent to us. We would stabilize the casualty, resuscitate as needed, give blood and/or IV fluids, and then medevac the casualty to a higher echelon of care after all life-saving measures had been instituted. We had no capability to hold casualties at the firebase due to a lack of space and resources, the need to make our trauma bays available to receive other casualties at a moment's notice, the unsanitary conditions, and ever-present need for surgical and other ongoing treatment.

Let me take a moment to discuss combat medicine. I spent years working in trauma centers where I was just down the hall from x-ray and lab resources, a short elevator ride from fully equipped operating rooms, and only a phone call away from virtually any specialist that I needed. No matter what type of trauma patient that presented to me in the ER I could avail myself of whatever ancillary services I needed, and any specialty back-up, within a matter of minutes—and all of this accomplished in a safe, clean, comfortable, climate-controlled environment. Now, picture being tasked with having to evaluate and treat severe life-threatening casualties in the desert, in 125 degree heat, in a tent with limited lighting, without x-ray or lab capability, and with the next closest higher level of medical facility or specialist being an hour away by helicopter—weather permitting. As daunting a task as that is, consider that you are not only just one physician but you may also be faced with multiple casualties arriving for treatment simultaneously with varying degrees of severity. That is what I had to deal with in the desert of Afghanistan and why you need well-trained members in your STP who can work well, and quickly, under that type of stressful condition.

A typical combat mission would unfold as follows:

> I would get word that we would be going outside the wire on a combat mission the following day and I was to report to the COC (Command Operations Center) tent for a briefing. We would meet in what we called the 'war room' which was a small GP tent that was off limits to any personnel who were not specifically invited to be there. It contained a large metal table comprised of a metal platform, usually used to transport heavy equipment by helicopter, which was supported on cinder blocks. There was a large map of Afghanistan that was spread out on the table. Hanging on one wall of the tent were flat screen TVs of topographical maps of the region. COL Kahn would generally conduct the briefing and usually say something to the effect, "Intel tells us that there is a band of Taliban amassing in this area (pointing to the map). We will be sending a convoy into the area, leaving at 0200 tomorrow morning. We figure they will probably ambush us around here (again pointing to the map)." It was never a question of IF they would ambush us but rather WHEN it would occur. The Marines have a strange way of doing business. We would decide how many vehicles we would need, which artillery to take, how many personnel (including one of us trauma docs and a few corpsmen), and how long we anticipated we would be gone. The missions generally lasted 3-4 days depending on how long it took for the enemy to engage us and how many times they would engage us along the way. The missions were generally up in the mountains and at some point the convoy would start receiving small arms

rifle fire, usually AK-47 rifle fire, and RPG rounds from some distance away up in the mountains. The convoy would then assume a defensive vehicle formation (called a herring bone configuration due to the positioning of the vehicles) and, after rapidly exiting the vehicles, everyone would return fire as our COMM operator called in the coordinates for an air strike. The firefight would continue until the Cobra or Apache AT-1 attack helicopters arrived and fired their missiles at the enemy position. It is a beautiful and welcome sight to see them at work effectively neutralizing the threat. Once the enemy fire stops then everyone moves forward climbing up to the enemy position to find mostly a scattering of body parts and dead bodies. Many of the enemy Taliban fighters would just be vaporized by the missiles. Any who did survive would be captured and flown back to FOB Ripley for questioning, usually after hours of time spent, by me, repairing their numerous shrapnel wounds and treating their burns. Any of our Marines who sustained casualties (usually gunshot wounds to the extremities not protected by body armor) would merely be pulled to a safe location and have only minimal medical care provided, such as a tourniquet to control bleeding, until the enemy threat was neutralized. This is referred to as 'medical care under fire.' Once the threat was neutralized then we would provide whatever care that we could in the field, called 'tactical medical care', and then transport the casualties back to the firebase either on the convoy (if it was ready to return to the base and they were medically stable), or via CH-53 or CH-46 helicopter to medevac them on a more urgent basis. Upon returning to the firebase there would be a de-briefing, then return to our usual routine until the next mission.

During one such mission the convoy was ambushed while traveling through a narrow canyon at the base of a mountain. As the firefight ensued one of our Marines was killed. After the enemy threat was neutralized by a barrage of Cobra helicopter missiles, there was only one Taliban fighter left alive. He had numerous shrapnel wounds and a portion of one of his ears, and part of an elbow, was blown off. He was transported back to our firebase and I spent several hours repairing his ear, elbow and multiple shrapnel wounds of his back and arms so he would be medically able to undergo interrogation as a PUC (Prisoner Under Custody). One of the most difficult duties I had, emotionally, was to provide medical care to the enemy after they had ambushed my fellow service members, particularly in this instance where we lost one of our own during the firefight involving this enemy combatant.

The following day we all got into formation at the firebase and held a short memorial service. It is a very somber, heart-wrenching, ceremony after losing one of our Marines in combat and knowing that there will be other battles ahead. There is an ever-present knowledge, and fear, that any one of us could be the recipient of the next memorial ceremony. I have attended more than I care to recall.

There is a particularly dangerous mission called a 'dust-off'. This entails flying a helicopter at high speed, close to the ground in order to present a more difficult target for the enemy to hit, into enemy territory, usually into the middle of an ongoing firefight, in order to pick-up a critically injured casualty for transport either back to the STP or on to a higher echelon of care, as in the case of an urgent surgical injury. The helicopter touches down in proximity to the injured Marine, usually in the midst of enemy fire, with the engines running and the propellers spinning. It is on the ground just long enough to load the casualty and immediately take-off. Due to the urgency of these missions, there is generally only a skeleton crew on-board consisting of the pilot, one crew member, a corpsman and a nurse or physician. During one such dust-off we had to medevac one of our Marines who had been shot through the thigh, which shattered his femur. It was bleeding profusely and progressively swelling. He was loaded into the helicopter, the leg was splinted, IVs were started and he was given pain medication as he was being transported to Charlie Med at Kandahar airbase for surgery. As we were taking off our helicopter started taking enemy fire. It was pitch black out and I had no NVGs (night vision goggles). There are two 50 cal. machine guns, one on either side of the helicopter. The flight crew member and myself each manned a machine gun to return fire as we took off to head for Kandahar. I would venture to say that there are probably not many physicians who have had the opportunity to fire a 50 cal. machine gun out of a CH-53 helicopter flying 100 feet off the ground in enemy territory. It is a real rush.

As was commonly the case, the trauma surgeon, CAPT Acosta, and the general surgeon, CAPT Baker were already in surgery when we arrived. COL Gonzalez, the orthopedic surgeon, took control of our Marine and I scrubbed-up to assist him in the repair. We were approximately halfway done with stabilizing the femur, having put a metal plate bridging the fragments on the back side of the femur, when another casualty was wheeled in requiring urgent orthopedic attention. Colonel Gonzalez looked at me and said, "You finish this" and then left to handle the new patient. Having assisted on orthopedic cases in the past, and having just had a nice refresher course assisting on this case, I went ahead and placed another plate over the front part of the femur fracture and then closed the muscle and fascia up through the 18 inch skin incision. While I was finishing my case, CAPT Acosta and CAPT Baker had completed their surgeries. As my patient was being transported to recovery three more casualties were brought into the OR. One was a gunshot wound to the chest that CAPT Acosta took. Another was a gunshot wound to the abdomen who looked seven months pregnant from bleeding into the abdominal cavity. The third was a gunshot wound through the thyroid cartilage (Adam's apple) leaving a large hole in the cartilage. All three were Taliban fighters. Since the third casualty had a viable airway, and was not actively bleeding, I scrubbed in with CAPT Baker to help find the source of internal bleeding in the abdominal gunshot patient. Once we controlled the bleeding, and resected a portion of damaged small intestine, I scrubbed-out and went to work on the third casualty. I had to do a neck dissection and repair some damaged muscle, as well as control some oozing blood vessels, before I could focus my attention on establishing a more viable airway. Once I had the neck muscle and vascular problems corrected, I trimmed the damaged thyroid cartilage and put in a tracheostomy tube through the already-present hole in the cartilage. I then cleaned up the neck wound as neatly as possible to allow for a permanent tracheostomy to be completed at some time in the near future. Having finished helping out at Charlie Med I went to bunk down in the hangar-style squad bay barracks to get some much-needed rest before I was to helo back to FOB Ripley the following day.

During the course of this combat deployment we had numerous mass casualty instances at our STP and the few patients that we did lose, due to being unsalvageable, were not any of our Marines. Most of the injuries incurred by our Marines were gunshot wounds from AK-47s and a majority of these were extremity wounds as a result of the trunk protection provided by our body armor. There is a substance called Quick Clot that is a granular material, resembling kitty litter, that causes blood to coagulate. It is very effective in stopping acute hemorrhage from large, open wounds that are continuously oozing, such as a leg amputation or a large tissue flap laid open by shrapnel. It is not intended to be used for gunshot wounds, however, because it plugs them up and they are difficult to repair until you clean out all of the Quick Clot. There was one corpsman who routinely packed gunshot wounds with the stuff despite my telling him not to do so. He happened to be one of the BAS corpsman. I nicknamed him QC and he eventually stopped doing it out of embarrassment when the nickname caught on and others started referring to him using that moniker.

I, and the members of my STP, treated over 1200 Afghan people during the course of my time in the combat theatre, and our STP treated over 500 casualties, mostly gunshot wounds to the extremities. There were a fair number of severely injured casualties but, fortunately, most of them were enemy forces. We lost one Marine during the entire deployment, which is one too many, but was a testament to the proficiency of our Marines. Some of the other units in our AO, such as army, Delta Force, Rangers, and Afghan National Army, were not so 'lucky'.

Towards the end of the deployment we spent ten days at the Kandahar Air base waiting for airlift to retrograde back to the U.S. We were basically just boarders there at that point. However, I was called out of my rack twice during the ten days to assist at Charlie Med for two mass casualty situations. The first was to assist in surgery, providing an extra set of hands so the surgeons could operate faster and get the casualties in and out of the OR in a more timely manner. The second mass casualty involved four Marines who were sitting across from each other in the back of a 7-ton truck that detonated an incendiary IED which blew up right beneath the bed of the truck where they were sitting. The ball of flame came up through the floor right in the middle of them. All four were burned over most of the front of their bodies. Myself, the other STP ER trauma physician, and the two surgeons each took a casualty and went to work debriding blistered second degree burns and controlling pain as best as possible. I kept cold, moist compresses over the entire front of my Marine, including his face, except for the area that I would be working on, for over three hours. He was in such pain that the frequent doses of IV morphine that I was giving him just wasn't controlling his pain. I was able to ultimately get a hold of the anesthesiologist to give him some IV sedation which took the edge off of his pain enough for me to finish my work. Once all of his burn areas were debrided, cleaned and dressed, we requested airlift medevac of the Marines to Landstuhl, Germany for treatment in their burn center. After I was finished dressing the burns on my 19-year-old Marine LCPL (Lance Corporal), I allowed two of his buddies to come in and keep him company while he was awaiting transport. They were standing to either side of him towards the head end of the gurney and I was standing directly at the head of the gurney. Although his face was bandaged, and he couldn't see me, I bent over and said to him, "Hi, I am LCDR Gilbert. I am the doctor who has been working on you for the past few hours." He said, "Fucker." A silence fell over everyone who was within earshot of him, and his two buddies turned white. Everyone looked at me to see what my reaction was going to be to being spoken to in that way by a LCPL, that being a potential Court Marshall offense. I just laughed, after which everyone else laughed, and all was good. He even chuckled a bit at that point. I assured him that he was going to be fine and I left to go get something to eat with my counterpart from the STP. Such is medicine in a war zone.

Nothing throughout your medical training, or even your years of medical practice in surgery and emergency medicine, really prepares you for what you face in combat. I spent years working in a trauma ER that saw 30,000 patients per year. Yet, the types of injuries that I saw and treated in combat—traumatic amputations of arms and legs from mines, mortars and IEDs, severe burns from incendiary IEDs, shrapnel wounds with the enormous amount of tissue destruction that they cause, although less in total number than all of the trauma that I treated in the ER, far surpassed anything that I was ever faced with--not to mention experiencing it in a place like Afghanistan with its oppressive heat, sand storms and, at times, while under enemy fire.

My time spent in Afghanistan was, without a doubt, the most physically and emotionally challenging and draining experience that I have ever had, or probably ever will again. With the possible exception of General Olson or General Abizaid, I believe that I was the oldest service member in our entire AO, and possibly all of Afghanistan. At 55 years of age there were times when between the heat, the sand storms, the mortar attacks, the ambushes, having to wear 50-60 lbs of gear while walking up in treacherous mountain terrain, putting in 19-hour days, sleeping on hard ground, dealing with all of the trauma in an austere environment without the typical reassurance of a trauma center within minutes, and the myriad other stressors to deal with, that I wondered to myself, "What in the hell are you doing here?" On the other hand, it was also the most rewarding, personally-fulfilling experience of my life-- helping to save lives, providing prompt medical care to our Marines in combat, bringing much-needed medical treatment (although rudimentary) to over 1200 Afghanis who get virtually no medical care, and being able to handle all of the challenges thrown my way.

There is an award that can only be earned while serving in combat called a Combat Action Ribbon. It is almost a rite of passage for a service member to qualify for receiving this award because it means that you are a true combat veteran. The qualification to receive, and wear, this ribbon are as follows:

"Active participation in ground or air combat during specifically listed military operations at which time he/she was under enemy fire and that his/her performance was satisfactory."

I am one of only a handful of physicians, serving in the active Reserve, who have been awarded this ribbon, which I wear with great pride.

The day we left Kandahar on our C-17 to return to the States it was 137 degrees. Since returning from Afghanistan, anytime I hear someone complain about the heat when it nears 100 degrees, or the weather in general, all I say is "Everything is relative".

When I returned home I wrote up an epidemiology report on data that I had been compiling during our time in Afghanistan. Contrary to what is a more typical situation, the dysentery rate among our Marines was only 0.47 per 1000 service members, which was extremely low. I feel that this was attributed in large part to the great job that our two PMTs (Preventive Medicine Techs) did. Unfortunately, the same cannot be said for the Afghan population that, due to poor hygiene and exposure to raw sewage, has a dysentery rate of 30-40% and is a major cause of infant and child death. Additionally, also due to the horrible living conditions and lack of medical care, 4% of babies die at birth, another 4-6% die within the first year of life, and another 2-3% die between the ages of 1 and 6.

I was more than happy to leave Afghanistan and return to the United States. The first stop that we made on U.S. soil, during our 36 hour flying ordeal back home, was to the airfield in Dover, Maine.

While we were there on the tarmac awaiting refueling we had the sobering experience of watching as a number of flag-draped coffins of fellow service members who had been KIA (Killed In Action) were being loaded into a C-17 aircraft for their final flight back to their families. We stood in silence, at attention, until all of the caskets were loaded onto the aircraft. What was going through my mind at the time, as I am sure was also the case with most everyone else in attendance, was 'there but for the grace of God go I'. We had survived our tour of duty and would be seeing our families within a few days. We had cheated the grim reaper.....so far.

Part of my STP, Kandahar, Afghanistan, 2004

Early stage of establishing our firebase, Afghanistan, 2004

Tent city before the 'graves' were dug, FOB Ripley, 2004

A typical 'grave' configuration, FOB Ripley, 2004

Our Command tent at FOB Ripley, 2004

A section of perimeter HESCO barrier, FOB Ripley, 2004

Our STP tents at FOB Ripley, 2004

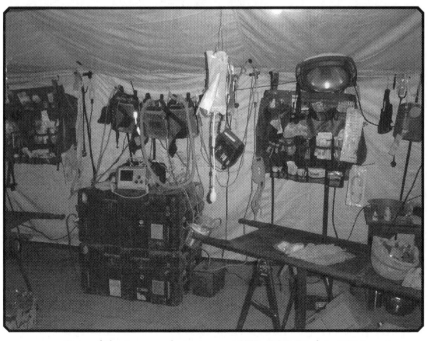

One of the trauma bays in our STP, FOB Ripley, 2004

Getting ready to leave on a combat mission, Afghanistan, 2004

Convoying on a combat mission, Afghanistan, 2004

One of many combat missions, Afghanistan, 2004

Taking a break during a mission, Afghanistan, 2004

A missile strike during an ambush, Afghanistan, 2004

A typical crowd of Afghan civilians awaiting
medical treatment, Afghanistan, 2004

Receiving casualties at our firebase, FOB Ripley, 2004

Repairing a gunshot wound in our STP, FOB Ripley, 2004

INCREASING COMMAND RESPONSIBILITY

In February of 2005 I was asked by our 4th Medical Battalion CO, CAPT Rom Stephens, to go to Norway to command the forward-embedded STP as part of a 15,000 member multi-national NATO training exercise, called Battle Griffin, near Antarctica. This entailed establishing a stationary field hospital approximately one hour north of Varness Air Base to provide medical support for the forces in the field that were moving north over a 60-mile stretch along the coast-- in knee-deep snow, with temperatures around minus 25 degrees. Our STP would provide the medical support for the forces as they moved along the coast. There would be cold weather combat training during the day, then the force would pack-up and move a certain distance at night and re-establish a bivouac site. Part of the STP would be assigned to the ground forces and the rest would be divided among the field hospital and a small contingent at Varness to handle day-to-day medical issues and provide sick call. As it was, it did provide for some excellent cold weather training for our STP.

The problem was that I had only been home a few months from two essentially back-to-back deployments and was not really interested in spending another month away from home—especially in such a cold environment. After voicing my reluctance to CAPT Stephens he assured me that if I agreed to go on this exercise he would not place any other demands on me for the foreseeable future.

So I agreed to go. It did turn out to be an excellent training exercise even with the brutal cold. When I returned home I was barely back in the States when I was approached by CAPT Stephens who told me that he wanted me to assume command of Det (Detachment) 1 in Tucson, AZ to provide some much-needed leadership and training. This would mean my leaving 4th Force Recon and having to fly to Tucson each month for my drill weekends. I was not particularly thrilled with this prospect, and reminded him about the promise he had made to me not to place any new demands on me if I agreed to serve with Battle Griffin. But CAPT Stephens could be rather persuasive and said that this could be a good career move for me. That being said, I agreed and, in April of 2005, I became the OIC of 4th Med BN, H&S Company, Detachment 1. I was now in command of that unit, as well as the primary STP for the 4th Marine Division, 4th MLG (Marine Logistics Group). At this point I was now regarded as the recognized subject matter expert on STPs due to all of my field and combat experience.

What I quickly discovered, upon assuming command of that detachment, was that CAPT Stephens was right. The members of that unit had significant military and medical knowledge and were actually incredibly motivated to utilize and expand on those skills. What they lacked was effective leadership. With the help of my hard-charging Det1 LPO (Lead Petty Officer) HM1Patrick Bunker, over the next two years I transformed Det 1 into the premiere detachment in H&S Company. Bunker was my right-hand man and I saw in him the potential to be a great leader in his own right. It is said, and my personal observations and experience confirm, that the senior enlisted actually run the military. They are the individuals who are directly superior to the junior enlisted and responsible for their day-to-day training, mentoring, and setting the example. Once in a while someone comes along who stands out among his peers and possesses the knowledge, skills, and ability to rise above the rest and perform all of those duties in an exemplary fashion. HM1 Bunker was, and is, such an individual. I recognized it almost immediately and capitalized upon it to the benefit of myself, himself, and, most importantly our junior enlisted. The more responsibility I gave him the more he shined. This was true not only at the detachment level but throughout the years that he served with me in my STP and at the Battalion Headquarters where I managed to orchestrate a change of billet in order to keep him by my side when my billet was changed to OIC of the 4th Med BN Headquarters Medical Detachment. In my opinion, he has done more for the enlisted members of our battalion than anyone; but more about him later. Under his direction, and mine, the corpsmen in our detachment progressed into a crackerjack military unit that became the core of my STP. Also during that time period, through the use of power point briefings that I had put together on subjects such as Trauma Fundamentals, Head Injuries, Penetrating Wounds, Burns, Blast Injuries, Heat Related Illness, Cold Weather Exposure, along with field exercises during which we would do mass casualty training, I honed the combat medical skills of my STP to ensure that it was mobilization-ready in preparation for anticipated future deployment.

In January of 2007, I was in the field on a training exercise with my STP at Miramar. When we returned to the Reserve Center I was called into the new CO, now CAPT John Williams, since CAPT Stephens had completed his two-year billet. He informed me that within a few days President Bush was going to be making an announcement authorizing a troop surge in Iraq to neutralize the increasing insurgency that had been evolving over the past year or so. He told me that I would be commanding the primary STP during the first wave of the surge. We were going to be situated at a small, remote, firebase in Western al Anbar Province--the current hotbed of insurgency activity. Some reports considered al Anbar province, which includes Baghdad, Ramadi, and Fallujah, to be un-winnable. We were going to be stationed at Camp Korean Village (Camp KV) which was a very small firebase just east of the Syrian border, around 200 miles due west of Baghdad, and just north of the highway linking Syria and Jordan with Baghdad--affectionately referred to as the 'Insurgency Corridor'. Our mission would be to provide casualty care for the anti-insurgency operations that would be going on in that region during the surge. I was ordered not to say anything to anyone until we received our 'Warning Orders', which are usually issued 1-2 months prior to our 'Mobilization Orders'. In the meantime I would be included in the planning of the mission which would involve hand-picking the members of my STP who would be deploying with me into combat. The core of that STP was my Tucson unit, Detachment 1, including my esteemed colleague and respected friend, HM1 Bunker. The unit was finally going to get to use the skills that they had been training so hard to perfect over the previous two years.

OFF TO WAR... YET AGAIN

I received my orders in June 2007 and, after going through my pre-mobilization processing for the third time in four years, I was off to Camp Lejuene, N.C. We had to spend some time at Camp Lejuene in order for those service members who needed it to receive some additional pre-mobilization training and to take care of any gear issues. Obviously, deploying was not new to me and, as far as any gear issues were concerned, I already had everything that I could possibly need to go virtually anywhere, anytime. In fact, as previously mentioned, I kept all of my gear in an old, no longer functioning, freezer--the kind that sits long ways on the floor with the door that lifts up. I could be ready to go within a matter of hours, if need be. The only thing that I needed to get at Camp Lejuene were some new canisters for my gas mask and the SAPI plate inserts for my flak vest to protect against AK-47 rounds and shrapnel. Aside from that, I was ready for another trip to the sand box.

Once all of the requisite training and out-processing was completed we were ready to mobilize out of Cherry Point, S.C. en route to Iraq via Kuwait, with a few refueling stops in between. We flew from Kuwait to al Asad, Iraq. From there we would helo to our firebase at Camp KV, following a few days of briefings. Not knowing what amenities, if any, would be available at our firebase spending a couple of days at a large base, such as al Asad, gave everyone a chance to purchase personal items to take with them in the event that we may not get another chance to do so for a while.

We were in the hangar area getting ready to board our CH-46 helicopter to take us to Camp Korean Village (KV) when I noticed a phone sitting on a counter. I decided to call home to say 'Hi', as it had been a few days since I had spoken to my family, and I did not know when I would have the next opportunity. I used the DSN line to route my call through Davis Montham Air Base, in Tucson, to my home in Reno, NV where it was then past midnight. My youngest daughter Anna answered the phone and I said, "Hi honey. I am getting ready to head out to our firebase and I am taking a minute to say hello before I leave." She broke down and, while choking back tears, somberly said, "We have been trying to get hold of you to tell you that grandpa (my father) died, yesterday." My heart sank because I knew that I was going to be the only trauma physician in a 200 mile radius and, as such, there was no way that I was going to be able to go home for the funeral. I literally had around two minutes to say my goodbyes to my family and then board our helicopter with this devastating news. There would be no time to go through any semblance of a normal grieving process and, since I was to be the only trauma physician in the region between Baghdad and Syria, I could not partake of the customary Red Cross family emergency leave usually afforded to service members whose family member dies while they are deployed. Not exactly the way you want to start a combat deployment.

Camp KV was in the middle of the desert surrounded by nothing but sand (nothing new to me) and the highway off into the distance. It was a small firebase but was very well fortified with firepower including Cobra At-1 attack helicopters, M1A1 Abrams tanks, LAVs (Light Armored Vehicles), MRAPs (Mine Resistant Armor Protected vehicles), LARs (Light Armored Reconnaissance vehicles), and numerous HUMVEES mounted with 30-Caliber machine guns. Another plus was that we were actually going to be in hard structures, made out of cinder blocks and plywood, rather than tents like I was used to, and there was a pretty darn nice chow hall where we could get hot food. There was even a small exchange on-base (another luxury that I was not used to having) where we could buy food, magazines, DVDs, CDs, personal items, tobacco products, certain gear items, etc. There was a limited selection, and not very well stocked, but it was certainly better than nothing. Overall, it was a pretty compact firebase but offered much more in the way of creature comforts than I was used to. Either way, it was going to be home for the next seven months.

Our STP worked out of two plywood structures, with corrugated roofs, which provided more protection from the elements than our usual GP (general purpose) tents. I had the core of my STP with me from my Tucson Det and we were augmented with additional personnel from some East Coast detachments and a unit out of Okinawa. The STP structures were a mess, and totally disorganized, so we set about to clean and reorganize everything to our specifications and re-supply whatever we needed to implement our level of practice. We revised the entire layout to make it more functional and ready to accept casualties. My XO, LCDR Steve Miller, and my LPO, HM1 Patrick Bunker, were invaluable to me during this organizational phase, and throughout the deployment, for that matter. Since one half of the STP had never met before our reorganizing mission/project it gave everyone an opportunity to get to know one another and lay the groundwork for working as a team in the treatment of combat casualties over the next seven months, as per our SOP. It also gave me a chance to observe and evaluate our new members and give some general combat medical briefings to the entire STP before the combat operations were in full gear.

With the firepower and troop strength that the surge provided things were turning around nicely in al Anbar province. The Iraqi people were getting fed-up with the insurgents, who were killing 100 Iraqis to every 1 coalition force, and were rallying behind our efforts by providing much of our useful intel. They were ratting on the insurgent strongholds--where they had their weapons arsenals and where they were making the IEDs. They even told our troops where the insurgents were hiding out. As a result, our forces were able to take the fight to the insurgents, raid and capture their weapons caches and bombs before they had a chance to use them, and cutoff their supply lines by having the troop strength to lock down each area as the insurgents were killed, captured, or driven out, thus preventing them from filtering back in like they were used to doing. Operations went so well that I treated far less casualties than I had in previous deployments, and very few serious ones involving our service members. The severest casualties were incurred by the insurgents and the Iraqi police, who were specifically targeted by the insurgents.

We maximized our down-time by hammering our corpsmen with hours and hours of combat medical training, FMF (Fleet Marine Force) training, mass casualty exercises, and mentoring to help prepare them for advancement exams for promotion. We also hosted monthly barbeques for the units in our proximity on-base to help maintain morale and camaraderie. My XO, LCDR Steven Miller, my PA, LCDR Michael Lettierre, my SEL (Senior Enlisted), HMC (Chief) Tom Ruffner, and my LPO, HM1 Patrick Bunker, were instrumental in keeping our operation running smoothly and overseeing all activities and our junior enlisted, in their assigned duties. Our administrative lead enlisted, HM2 John Howe and our squad leaders, HM1 Chris Davila, HM1 Andrew Pashos, and HM2 Sarah Moore, were the hands-on leaders of our junior enlisted, overseeing all of the day to day collateral duties, watch duties, and work details.

I conducted formations and ceremonies for occasions such as September 11th, the Navy birthday (October 13th), the Marine Corps birthday (November 10th), and Veteran's Day. We celebrated Thanksgiving, Christmas and New Years as best we could, given our circumstances. Because I had been promoted to Commander in July of 2007, I was the most senior ranking officer on base and had the honor of officiating at several promotion and re-enlistment formations. These were some of my favorite functions, since I always like to recognize our enlisted when they achieve a promotion. I found them extremely gratifying to conduct for any of our enlisted who decide to re-enlist in order to extend their commitment to the armed forces, particularly while we are at war, and with the very likely prospect of future deployments.

Additionally, while in theatre, we took on another challenge. There is a device called the Fleet Marine Force Warfare Device that is awarded to Navy personnel who complete a rigorous course of training in 23 areas of instruction including, but not limited to, Mission, Organization and Fundamentals, Combat Leadership Fundamentals, Security Fundamentals, Field Communications Fundamentals, Weapons Fundamentals, Land Navigation Fundamentals, Infantry Fundamentals, Light Armored Reconnaissance (LAR) Fundamentals, Ground Command Element Fundamentals, and Air Command Element Fundamentals, and one of my personal favorites, Marine Corps History-- to mention just a few. In order to qualify for this device you had to complete all of the course instruction in each section and get signed off for successful completion of each section. In addition to completing all of the didactic and field training you had to also complete a 6-mile hike with full pack. After all of this you take a comprehensive written exam that tests you on all 23 sections of the FMF Training book and, upon successfully passing that exam, you then have to sit before a Board for an oral exam, as well, during which you are questioned by 3-5 Board members on all of the sections. If you successfully complete, and pass, all of this you are then awarded the device which you can proudly wear on your uniform above your ribbons or above your left breast pocket on your BDUs (cammies). This is a very prestigious award to earn since any Navy personnel who has the device is recognized as a subject matter expert in all things Marine Corps and is forever bonded to the Marine Corps. It also shows their degree of commitment to the Corps in the case of those who are serving with the Marines, such as in Program 9.

This device had only been offered to naval officers since 2006 and I am proud to say that in 2007 I was one of the first to qualify for the award while in combat in Iraq. I am also proud to say that my entire STP also successfully completed all of the training and passed the written and oral exams on their first try--the first time that an entire unit had achieved a 100% pass rate.

Before an enlisted service member can be promoted they have to first qualify for, and then pass, an advancement exam. These comprehensive exams are intentionally quite difficult so that only those who are deserving of promotion receive that promotion. I had six members of my STP come up for promotion while we were in Iraq and I am proud to say that every one of them passed their advancement exam on their first attempt. This is also very uncommon and a testament to both their drive and commitment, but also to the excellent coaching and training that they received by my senior enlisted members.

All in all, we had a very successful, rewarding deployment on many fronts. The surge was a tremendous success with al Anbar Province, which was considered unwinnable, now the safest province in Iraq. Amazingly, and blessed to report, we lost none of our Marines during combat operations and none of the civilian casualties that we treated. We had a 100% pass rate on the FMF Warfare Device and Advancement exams and myself, along with my XO, my senior enlisted members, and my physician assistant, LCDR Mike Lettiere, provided our junior enlisted STP members with some of the best training that they will ever receive. Like a proud 'papa', I am pleased to say they will be prepared to serve anywhere in the world and be confident in their abilities as corpsmen.

It was not the most combat-intense deployment (which was a good thing), nor did we treat as many severe casualties as I had in previous deployments--which is, perhaps, an even better thing. But I would have to say that it was a gratifying, enriching experience for me and a tremendous learning and maturing experience for the members of my STP.....and that is all that any commanding officer can hope for at the end of the day.

The core of my 4th Medical Battalion STP

My STP in Iraq, 2007/2008

Some of our fire power at Camp KV, Iraq, 2007/2008

More fire power

In full battle-rattle, getting ready for a mission in Iraq, 2007/2008

The core of my Iraq STP sharing some R&R during our retrograde back to the U.S. following the surge in Iraq, 2007/2008

HOMEWARD BOUND... ONCE AGAIN

By mid-March, 2008 we were ready to begin the retrograde process back to the States. The RIP (Replacement In Personnel) was complete and our replacements were settled in and well-oriented to the base and the SOPs. Due to the success of the surge, al Anbar province, once considered 'unwinnable' by many in the intelligence agencies, was now the safest province in all of Iraq. In seven months in theatre our STP had its lowest volume of casualties in any deployment thus far--the vast majority were relatively minor, with only a scattering of serious injuries. Due to the number of personnel leaving the firebase the retrograde process was done in three phases. I purposely stayed behind to be in the last group to leave the base along with a few members of my STP, including my right hand man, HM1 Bunker. All of the other personnel had convoyed back to al Asad but, since there was only a small contingent of us awaiting departure, it was decided to fly us back to al Asad, rather than put a convoy together for such a small group. As we were standing on the tarmac getting ready to board one of the new MV-22 Ospreys, that was going to take us back to al Asad, I turned to my LPO, HM1 Bunker and, with a heart lighter than it had been in 7 months, said, "Let's go home, HM1."

We arrived back at Cherry Point, S.C. on Wednesday of Holy Week and took buses back to Camp Lejuene so we could go through the demobilization process and head back to our families. What we found out, to our dismay, was that the base was going to begin its 96-hour holiday leave in two days which meant that, after being gone for the past nine months, the vast majority of us were not going to be able to return home before Easter. The demob process takes a minimum of three days but can be accomplished in two days if everything is in perfect order, and the processing personnel are uncharacteristically motivated. The likelihood of both of those things happening in concert was slim to none.

The first part of the check-out process is to obtain your service and medical records from the processing center to carry with you for each step of the demob process. You have to be signed off by medical, dental, psych, chaplain, and VA benefits. The admin staff then updates your service record and completes your DD214 form which documents your dates of deployment and your list of previously earned ribbons and medals, as well as any new ones that you are entitled to from your current deployment. Interspersed with all of this are briefs that are given by legal services and a social worker, who talks to you in groups about sexual harassment/abuse issues, in case anyone had problems in that regard while on deployment. There are also a number of forms that have to be filled out. Once all of this is completed, and all of the appropriate signatures have been obtained, you are then sent to the travel desk to get your airline reservation made so you can leave, usually within the next 24 hours.

After our bus ride from Cherry Point to Camp Lejuene we took all of our gear to our temporary barracks. After turning in our weapons at the armory we went to the processing center to pick-up our records. When they had finished handing out everyone's records the only person not to receive theirs was yours truly. I went inside to ask the admin staff member in charge where my records were and I was informed that they were retaining mine for right now because they may be short one trauma physician and they may have to turn me around and send me back to Iraq. I won't tell you what I said but it wasn't "Aw, shucks." I was told to check back on the Tuesday after Easter by which time they should be able to tell me whether or not I was going home or back to Iraq. When I called home to tell my wife, Debby, that I wouldn't be home for Easter I didn't have the heart to tell her that I may be going back to Iraq. I basically told her that the soonest I would be able to begin my demob process would be the Tuesday after Easter, which was, hopefully, the truth. Although I was not going to be able to get home before Easter, I pushed the demob personnel to the limit to insure that as many of my troops would get home as possible. Fortunately, we were able to get a large number of our battalion on planes headed home within a couple of days.

Luck was with me when I returned to the processing center on Tuesday morning. I was handed my records and told that the physician situation in Iraq had been resolved—I was going home. The members of our battalion who were not lucky enough to get out of Camp Lejuene over Easter weekend were, for the most part, going to leave for home on that Tuesday. That left just me and a small contingent of stragglers in the final stages of their demob process. After the enlisted clerk handed me my records I decided to pull rank and said, "I want to be out of here by tomorrow and I need you to make it happen." He said, "Yes, sir." Needless to say, I had a rather abridged check-out process. I had a brief interface with all of the pertinent players and was whisked through medical and dental screening. Having turned a 3-day process into a 1-day process I was ready to fly home on Wednesday. My family, who I had not seen in nine months, were all waiting for me at the security checkpoint at the end of the long hallway leading from the gates to baggage claim. They were certainly a welcome sight to me.

When I left for deployment in June of 2007 my granddaughter, Carmella, was only sixteen months old. She was my "Little Peanut" and she sure loved her Papa. I had missed the wedding of my youngest daughter Anna to a guy I had only met over WebCam, after a short whirlwind romance. I had also missed a couple of my son Joey's boxing matches. There is always an adjustment period for both service members and their families upon returning home from war, particularly after a 9-month hiatus. It doesn't matter if you are fifty-eight or two. It took Carmella less than a week to warm-up to me again and rekindle the closeness that we had when I left.

Approximately one week after I had returned home my wife, Carmella, and I were walking down the road that runs along the property line of our ranch. As we were walking my wife said to Carmella, "Isn't it nice having Papa back home again?" Carmella stopped dead in her tracks and turned towards me. That little two-foot tall, two-year old, got a serious look on her face, pointed her finger up at me, and as she shook it at me she said, "And you are never leaving home again!" Only time will tell if she is right.

SO WHY DO WE DO IT?

It is reasonable to say that every time that I have been deployed overseas I have probably been one of the oldest service members in-country and, certainly, in the combat AO. The CGs (Commanding Generals) of the various military forces in Iraq and Afghanistan may have been around my age but as far as those of us with boots on the ground in actual combat.....I was probably one of the, if not the, oldest. I have been asked many times, since 2003, by many individuals—"Why do you continue to serve with the Marines, knowing that places you at risk for more deployments?" The point being, I could have either left the Reserves at any point or, if I wanted to stay in the Reserves but remain out of harm's way, I could have left Program 9 (Marine medical) and returned to the blue side medical (Navy) where I would have been reassigned to a Navy medical detachment at some Reserve Center and resumed my pre-2004 status. You see, with rare exception, the only naval personnel who actually get deployed into combat are those serving with Program 9. Typically, when a naval physician gets called into active duty service during a conflict he or she generally gets sent either to a safe base within the U.S. or Europe or, at worst, may get sent to one of the large bases in Iraq or Afghanistan to work at a MTF (Medical Treatment Facility) within the safe confines of the large base.

One of the key reasons anyone continues to serve in the Marine Corps is a life-long bond that forms between Marines as a result of the training, traditions, history, combat experience and overall esprit de corps that is the Marine Corps. It is hard to explain to someone who has not been a part of that but it is undeniable. For me, personally, there were many other reasons why I chose to continue to serve and put myself in harms' way as many times as I did. Just a few examples:

Everyone knows of the reputation that the Marine Corps has for being a well-disciplined, well-trained, extremely tough, universally respected fighting force. Well, that doesn't just happen by itself. I spent years training and serving with Marines, from raw recruits on up to battalion commanders, on drill weekends, brutal field exercises, and, of course, combat deployments. Keep in mind that everyone who serves in the Armed Forces of the United States does so by choice. It is totally voluntary since there is no longer a draft. When I would look around and see how hard these 19 and 20 year old Marines would train, and put their lives on the line for their Country, when they could be hanging out with their friends at the mall or the movie theatre (as opposed to the combat theatre) or just doing a million other non life-threatening activities, I figured that the least that I could do was provide them with the best possible medical care within my power.

I was actually injured during my combat tour in Afghanistan in 2004. I injured my left hip jumping out of the back of a 7-ton truck while on a convoy into the mountains of Afghanistan during a combat mission. When a convoy gets ambushed everyone bales out of the vehicles as quickly as possible to take-up defensive positions and avoid significant combat casualties that would occur if a loaded truck was to get struck by an RPG (Rocket Propelled Grenade). When you are in full combat gear you are wearing and/or carrying around 65lbs of excess weight. The tailgate of a 7-ton is close to 8 feet off the ground. When I jumped down from the back of the truck I landed straight-legged on my left leg which caused severe, sharp pain in my left hip that seemed to shoot up through the top of my head. There was nothing that I could do about it at the time since we were on a combat mission and I was the only trauma physician in the whole combat AO. The immediate pain gradually subsided and I took ibuprofen, whenever I had a chance, over the next couple of weeks until the pain gradually went away. Within a couple of years I began to notice recurring pain in my left hip which was getting gradually worse. At my wife's insistence I went to see a hip specialist, in the summer of 2006, who examined me and took x-rays. He told me that I basically had bone-on-bone in my left hip and I needed a total hip replacement. I told him that it was not an option because I was fairly certain that our battalion would be going back to Iraq sooner than later and I knew that having a total hip replacement would probably render me non-deployable for combat. So I pretty much just lived with the pain and, sure enough, we were called up for a combat deployment to Iraq for the surge in 2007, as previously addressed earlier in this book. There was one small catch, however.....

.....It is customary before any large combat deployment for the military forces to undergo pre-deployment training and briefings, specific to the particular mission. Relative to this deployment for the surge our training was to take place at Quantico, in Virginia. This training was totally separate and apart from any immediate pre-deployment training that would occur at our mobilization site prior to leaving OCONUS (overseas). The training entailed field exercises, night ops, weapons qualifications, and a multitude of briefings. Twice a year, usually in April and October, we underwent our PRT which involved doing push-ups, sit-ups, pull-ups and a 3-mile run. All of these required that you do a minimum of repetitions within 2 minutes and, in the case of the 3-mile run, finish the run within a certain time limit. If you failed any of the components you were determined to be NPQ (Not Physically Qualified) and would thus flunk that PRT cycle. If you flunked three such cycles in a row you would be Administratively Separated from the Marine Corps and flunking even one cycle would render you non-deployable. So herein lay the problem:

It had been six months since the last PRT cycle and I barely passed the run portion. I had no problem doing the push-ups, sit-ups and pull-ups but the run was a killer—literally, as the pain was nearly unbearable while running. By the time we were at Quantico I had pain in my hip with every step I took and when I ran it felt like someone was sticking a spike into my hip every time I came down on my left foot. Now I was there at Quantico preparing to go into combat with 300 Marines from my battalion and most of them knew that I had a bad hip but everyone basically looked the other way and, as long as I could pass the PRT, and keep up with all of the training, no one made an issue of it…..until now. They all knew that if I didn't pass this PRT cycle I would not be able to deploy with them and they would have to find another trauma specialist to go into combat with them, most-likely someone who they did not know and who, in all likelihood, did not have the combat experience that I had, or the knowledge of Shock Trauma Platoons.

It was now time for the run to begin. It was a 3-mile course that started over an open field approximately ¼ mile across and then continued into the forest. It wound through the trees for around 2 ½ miles and then exited back across the field to the start/finish. So 300 of us took off running and once we entered the forest it was hard to tell where you were in the pack due to the dense trees. All I knew was that every time my left foot struck the ground it sent a jolt of pain through my hip. As I was nearing the spot where the trail exits the trees and opens onto the field four marines appeared in view heading right for me. Two of them got on each side of me and one of them said "Sir, if you don't pick-up the pace you are not going to make your time." At hearing that I took off at a dead run, flanked by the Marines, and we sprinted across the field where I saw all of the other Marines gathered together yelling OOORAH!, OOORAH!, OOORAH! This really motivated me and I basically just ignored the pain and ran even faster. I finished the run barely within the time allotted and everyone was cheering. It was probably one of the most uplifting moments of my life and re-enforced why I continued to serve with the greatest fighting force on earth.

I will give you one other personal example to illustrate why serving with the Marines was such a worthwhile experience. If you will recall, I was placed in command of 4th Med BN, Det 1 back in 2005 at the insistence of our battalion CO. I had spent three years in command of that unit and had transformed it into an exemplary medical unit and the core of my STP. Every member of that unit had become corpsmen of which I could not be more proud, and who I would put up against any other corpsman in regards to skill, discipline, spirit, and motivation. We were truly a well-oiled machine. But after those three years I was ordered by our Command to change billets and to take over command of the Headquarters Medical Detachment at Miramar Marine Base in San Diego. On our last drill weekend together I took the whole unit out for pizza and we said our goodbyes, only to see each other on future STP field exercises or if we were to ever deploy together again.

Several months later a package arrived for me in the mail. In the box were two large framed pictures in very nice frames. One was of our unit that was taken at dusk while out on patrol in Iraq. The other was of the USS Arizona Memorial at Pearl Harbor because they knew how moved I was when I visited the memorial some years previous. I thought to myself that this was a really nice gesture on their part until I happened to glance at the back of the framed pictures where they had all written personal notes to me, as well as quotes of things that I had said to them over the years that had stuck in their minds. Now I was getting choked up and when I thought I couldn't be more gratified I found a typed letter in the box that had contained the pictures. This is what it said:

CDR Gilbert,

Please accept these pictures as a small token of our appreciation for all that you have done for the sailors of the detachment, the NOSC and the Company. It is very difficult to put into words what your Leadership, Experience and Friendship has meant to us. You have improved every one of us on a personal and a professional level.

We certainly hope that every time you look at these pictures you will think of us and the time you spent in

Tucson. Just like any relationship there is more than meets the eye. We have put quotes on the back that remind us of you. So when people look at the pictures they will only be seeing part of the story. Only a select few will know what's on the back.

Our OIC's and personnel will come and go. Please understand that there will only be one Skipper of the Tucson Det; that is you. No matter what the circumstances come our way we will always strive to meet your level of commitment and standards. One of the many things we have learned from you is that Honor, Courage and Commitment is more than a recruiting slogan, but words we should all live by.

Sir, you keep Leading from the FRONT, no need to look behind you for Tucson Det 1 will always have your back

Very Respectfully,

Tucson Detachment One, H&S Company, 4th Medical Battalion, 4th Marine Logistics Group

Anyone who really knows me will attest to the fact that I am not the most emotional guy in the world. But I have to admit that as I was reading that letter my eyes welled up with tears and re-enforced what I knew in my heart to be true, that what I had done in service to my Country, and the members of its armed forces, was worthwhile and worth continuing to do for the foreseeable future.

The above examples are but a few that illustrate why I took on the challenges and put my mind and body through as much as I did for however long I did it. There is no question that the time I spent on combat deployments, especially in Afghanistan, were the most emotionally and physically stressful and demanding periods of time in my entire life; but at the same time, also the most rewarding.

I will carry and cherish the memories, both good and bad, as well as the lifelong friendships that I have made, with me for the rest of my days. I have no regrets and my love for our Country and the Corps is steadfast and something that I wear with pride.

I retired from the military in April of 2012, not because I would have had to obtain an age waiver to stay in the military, as many people thought, but for a personal/practical reason. Having finally had my hip replacement surgery, after returning home from Iraq in 2008, I knew in my heart that I should probably not deploy again into a ground combat situation because if I had to jump out of the back of another 7-ton truck during an ambush, and happen to land on my left leg the way I did when I was in Afghanistan, I could very easily shatter my femur which would then not only make ME a casualty but would also leave my fellow troops without their trauma doc. So I decided to hang it up. Now, I could have also left Program 9 and returned to the blue side Navy medical where I would have been safe from the prospect of being sent into harm's way. But after serving with the Marines as long as I did, and under the circumstances that I did, I just could not see myself as becoming what we in the Marine Corps affectionately call a REMF. The RE stands for Rear Echelon. You can probably surmise what the MF stands for.

Most everyone has heard the saying 'Once a Marine, Always a Marine'. This is certainly true for all of the reasons that I have previously alluded to but there is another more palpable and concrete reason. Everyone who serves with the Marines has what is called their MOS. It is what you do in your service e.g. infantry, communications, motor-T, engineering, intel, personnel, etc., or, as in my case, ER trauma specialist. If you have a critical MOS, meaning either the service that you provide to the Marine corps is in short supply or in very high demand, or both, as in my case, than if an important combat mission arises that requires the services of someone in one of the critical MOS's the Marines corps will fill that need, even if it means calling up someone out of 'retirement' and back into service. When I joined the 4th Medical Battalion, and assumed command of its primary Shock Trauma Platoon, there were 4 standing STPs and

8 ER trauma physicians. By the time I retired in 2012 there were only 2 STPs and only 3 ER trauma physicians, none of whom had any combat experience. Fortunately, there were two new ER trauma physicians who were joining our battalion as I was retiring which made me somewhat less anxious, and guilty, about leaving. They had no combat experience either but, hopefully, they will never need any.

The world is not a nice place and there is ongoing turmoil throughout the Middle East, not to mention North Korea and Africa. There is always the very real possibility for any of those volatile areas to erupt and necessitate a major ground combat operation that would, most certainly, include the Marine Corps.....and the Marines never go into combat without an STP. Knowing how important it is, for mission success, to have the most able-bodied, combat-seasoned, proficient assets, as part of any combat operation, it brings to mind that day in April, 2008 when I had just gotten home from my 9-month combat tour of duty in Iraq and I was walking down that road with my wife and my then 26-month old granddaughter. I remember her reply to my wife's question "Isn't it nice having Papa back home again?" as she pointed her finger at me, saying, "And you are never leaving home again!"

Time will tell.....time will tell.

THANK YOU

To my wife, Debby, for being the consummate military wife, her years of support during my service, and her unselfish, devoted care of our home and family in my absence. Also to my family and friends, for their support and encouragement throughout my military career.